PUFFIN BOOKS

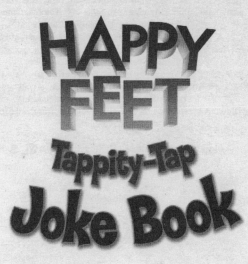

# HAPPY FEET
## Tappity-Tap
## Joke Book

PUFFIN BOOKS

Published by the Penguin Group
Penguin Books Ltd, 80 Strand, London WC2R 0RL, England
Penguin Group (USA) Inc., 375 Hudson Street, New York, New York 10014, USA
Penguin Group (Canada), 90 Eglinton Avenue East, Suite 700, Toronto, Ontario, Canada M4P 2Y3
(a division of Pearson Penguin Canada Inc.)
Penguin Ireland, 25 St Stephen's Green, Dublin 2, Ireland (a division of Penguin Books Ltd)
Penguin Group (Australia), 250 Camberwell Road, Camberwell, Victoria 3124, Australia
(a division of Pearson Australia Group Pty Ltd)
Penguin Books India Pvt Ltd, 11 Community Centre, Panchsheel Park, New Delhi – 110 017, India
Penguin Group (NZ), cnr Airborne and Rosedale Roads, Albany, Auckland 1310, New Zealand
(a division of Pearson New Zealand Ltd)
Penguin Books (South Africa) (Pty) Ltd, 24 Sturdee Avenue, Rosebank, Johannesburg 2196,
South Africa

Penguin Books Ltd, Registered Offices: 80 Strand, London WC2R 0RL, England

penguin.com

First published 2006

PEUK 4692

Written by Richard Dungworth
All rights reserved

Made and printed in England by Clays Ltd, St Ives plc

British Library Cataloguing in Publication Data
A CIP catalogue record for this book is available from the British Library

ISBN-13: 978–0–141–32144–8
ISBN-10: 0–141–32144–X

# HAPPY FEET
## Tappity-Tap
# Joke Book

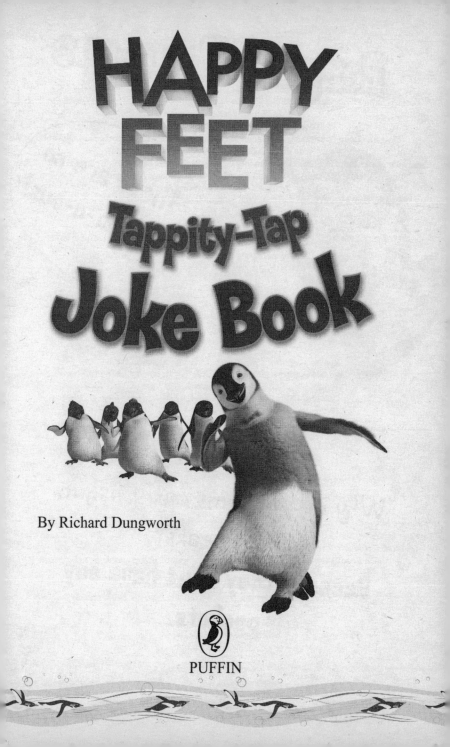

By Richard Dungworth

PUFFIN

Why do penguins carry fish in their beaks?
Because they don't have any pockets.

What's black and white with
twenty-two flippers?
**Penguin United.**

What kind of penguin has one
leg and plays electric guitar?
**A rockhopper penguin.**

What did the
penguin say to
the fish?
**'Catch you later!'**

# Cool Antarctic Jokes

Top jokes from the bottom of the world!

What's the best-selling cereal in the Antarctic? **Ice Crispies.**

Why is it impossible to feel low
at the South Pole?
**Because the only way is up.**

Which stroke should you swim
in the Antarctic Ocean?
**Freeze-style.**

Do penguins and polar bears
have much in common?
**No - they're poles apart.**

Tap-Tap
Tippity Tap
Tap-Tap

What Mexican speciality is
served in the Antarctic?
**Brrr-itos with chilli.**

# Gloria's Penguin Pop Pages

Here's my pick of the Heartsong Charts . . .

**NUMBER ONE IN THE ADELIE PENGUIN CHART**

'Mi Chico Latino'
Geri Halliwell

**FAVOURITE PENGUIN BAND**

McDon'tFly

# FLiPPER-TASTiC HiTS

'That's My Shoal' Shayne Ward

'The Tide Is High' Atomic Kitten

'Beak Like Me' Sugarbabes

'I Believe I Can Fly' R. Kelly

'Frozen' Madonna

'Flying Without Wings' Westlife

# CHART-TOPPING ANTARCTIC ACTS

**Gulls Aloud**

**Vestlife**

**Coldplay**

**Ice Girls**

**Shivababes**

**Seal**

# Mumble's Dance Jokes

These'll put the ha-ha-ha in your cha-cha-cha!

What's the best dance to do in the Antarctic? **The rum-brrrrrr.**

What do you call penguins who can rock and roll underwater? **Deep-sea jivers.**

**MUMBLE:** I think I'm going to give up tap-dancing, Dad.

**MEMPHIS:** Why, son?

**MUMBLE:** I keep falling in the sink!

Which Irish dance spectacular was a smash Antarctic hit?

**Shiverdance.**

How do love-struck young penguins dance?

**Chick to chick.**

# Penguin Screamers

What do penguins sing at a birthday party?
**'Freeze A Jolly Good Fellow.'**

What do you call a penguin in the desert?
**Lost.**

What's black and white and tells cheesy jokes?
**A pun-guin.**

What do laid-back penguins do at the weekend? **Just go with the floe.**

What do you call a penguin with no eyes? **A pengun.**

... Then there was the penguin who always liked to land the biggest catch. **His friends got fed up with him fishing for compliments.**

Where do fish go on holiday? **Finland.**

What fish goes best with ice-cream? **Jellyfish.**

Thought For The Day: **Why are fish so dumb when they live in schools?**

# Ask Lovelace

**Got a problem? Bring it on . . .**

REMEMBER:
One pebble,
one question.

**ELEPHANT SEAL:**
What's good for excessive wind, O Enlightened One.
**LOVELACE:**
A kite, fool!

**ADELIE PENGUIN:**
O Serene One, I swallowed some of my feathers while preening. Will I be OK?
**LOVELACE:**
You might feel a little down in the mouth.

**ADELIE PENGUIN:** Señor Lovelace, the two penguins I share a nest with keep on falling out. What should I do?

**LOVELACE:** *Friend, build a bigger nest!*

**GLORIA:**
We have . . . tra-la, tra-la-la.

**MUMBLE:**
tap-tippity-tap.

**GLORIA:**
. . . a question . . . fa-la-la-la-lah.

**MUMBLE:**
tap-whisssshhhh-chippita-chippita.

**GLORIA:**
. . . for you, shoo-bee-doo-bee-doo.

**LOVELACE:**
OK, OK – *ain't no need to make a song and dance about it!*

# Chick Chuckles

Loving these jokes, *amigos!*

What do you call an unhatched penguin chick?
**Shell-ey.**

What's the difference between a human child and a penguin chick?
**A child grows up, but a chick grows down.**

Which American city do baby penguins most want to live in?
**Chick-ago.**

What do you call it when a mother penguin has three chicks?
**A hatch-trick.**

Where do you pay for a baby penguin?
**At the chick-out.**

# Seabird Jokes

**Enough awredy wiv de flipper-boid jokes!**

Which seabirds make the best kebabs?

**Skuas.**

What do you call a large, bad-tempered seabird?

**An alba-cross.**

What seabird is always out of breath?
**A puffin.**

Then there was the man arrested for stealing seabirds.
**He claimed he'd been taught to always take terns.**

Which seabirds are best at knots?
**Gull guides.**

# Wise Words From the Emperor Elders

Don't count your chicks until they've hatched.

Let sleeping seals lie.

Maintain a strict seafood diet.
If you see food, eat it.

Remember: we all get down.

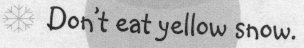 Don't eat yellow snow.

Pebbles can't buy you love.

There aren't plenty more
fish in the sea.

# Whale Jokes

You gonna *whale* with laughter, muchachos!

What do you call a baby whale?
**A little squirt.**

What's huge, squirts water, and is very useful in the garden?
**A whale-barrow.**

Where would you weigh a whale?
**At a whale-weigh station.**

What do you call a bunch of killer
whales playing classical music?
**An orca-stra.**

# Penguin Howlers

What's big and fat, lives in jungle
rivers, and has limbs like a penguin?
**A flipper-potamus.**

What does Miss Viola give her
pupils for good work?
**An Antarc-tick.**

Why shouldn't you trust penguins?
**There's something a bit fishy about them.**

How do penguins communicate over long distances?
**By walky-squawky.**

What do penguins do when it's really cold?
**Just chill.**

# Mrs Astrakhan's Singing Jokes

These will make your heart sink!

What's the best thing to do at singing lessons? **Take notes.**

What trousers can improve your singing? **Vocal cords.**

# The Black and White Section

What's black and white and blue?
**A depressed penguin.**

What's black and white and yellow?
**A cowardly penguin.**

What's black and white and green?
**A penguin on a rollercoaster.**

What's black and white and purple?
**A penguin holding its breath.**

What's black and white
and black and white?
**A penguin in a tuxedo.**

What's black and white and black
and white and black and white?
**A penguin rolling down a hill.**

What's black and white
and red all over?
**An embarrassed zebra in the
wrong joke book.**

# Ask Lovelace

Feel the lurve, brothers and sisters . . .

REMEMBER:
One pebble,
one question.

**ADELIE PENGUIN:**
Guru, O Guru, I keep thinking I'm a fish!

*LOVELACE:*

*Relax, friend. It's a common-plaice problem.*

**ADELIE PENGUIN:** O Wise One, I'm being bothered by a rude one-legged male. What should I do?

**LOVELACE:** Tell him to hop it, sister!

**ADELIE PENGUIN:** Aiy! I can't fly! I can't fly! What should I do, Señor Lovelace!

**LOVELACE:** Don't get in such a flap, fool!

**ADELIE PENGUIN:** I accidentally swallowed a pebble. How will I feel when it comes out?

**LOVELACE:** You'll be rock bottom, my man.

# Seal Squealers

Why are Elephant seals
so wrinkled?
**Have you ever tried ironing one?**

Why are Leopard seals no good
at hide-and-seek?
**Because they're always spotted.**

**Try these on
ol' lard-faced
whiskery
Rubber-butt!**

Why is an Elephant seal big, brown and lumpy?
**Because if it was small, white and smooth he'd be an aspirin.**

What do you call three haddock and a side order of Adelie penguin?
**A seal meal deal.**

Where do baby seals come from?
**New Seal-land.**

# Penguin Jokes

What do you call an unlucky penguin?

**A peng-lose.**

Where do Emperor penguins go to vote?

**The South Poll.**

Which of Gloria's suitors has the best eyesight?

**Seymour.**

What do penguins have that no other animal does?

**Baby penguins.**

What's black and white, with flippers, and swims in the sea?
**A scuba-diving zebra.**

# Deep-sea Jokes

Oi *caramba* – these babies are *deeply* funny!

**NORMA JEAN:** Hey, honey – what lies at the bottom of the sea and shivers?

**MEMPHIS:** I don't know, sugar.

**NORMA JEAN:** A nervous wreck!

How do penguins get along together underwater?
**Swimmingly.**

Hey, *hombre* - how ju dig a hole in the ocean floor?

I don't know - how?

With a pneumatic krill!

What do penguins get when they graduate in deep-sea fishing?
**A deep-loma.**

What kind of food do you find at the bottom of the Antarctic Ocean?
**Deep-frozen.**

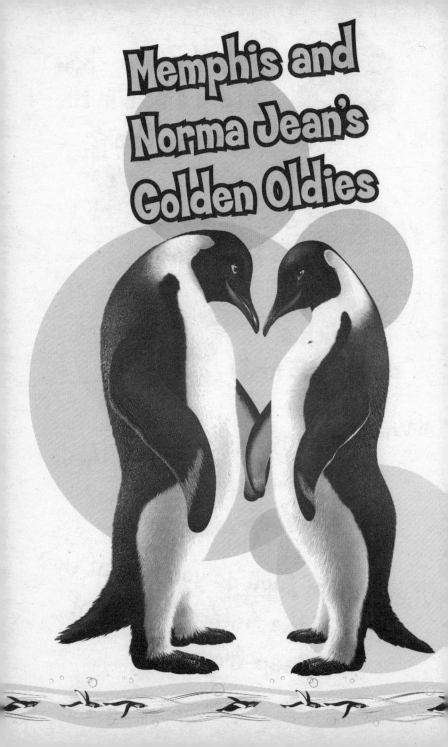

Memphis and
Norma Jean's
Golden Oldies

'Waddle, I Do'

'On the Sleet Where You Live'

'We Don't Squawk Any More'

'Don't Preen Me This Way'

'Leader of the Pack Ice'

'Undefrostable'

'You'll Never Squawk Alone'

'I Only Have Ice for You'

'Beak It'

'Ice Ice Baby'

# More Seabird Jokes

I figure you desoive some more . . .

Where do Antarctic seabirds fill up?
**At a petrel station.**

What do you call a wonky seabird?
**Skua-whiff.**

Do seabirds like rubies or opals? **Neither – diamonds are a gull's best friend.**

What do you call a man with a seabird on his head? **Cliff.**

What's a skua's favourite meal? **Fish 'n' chicks.**

How many Adelie penguins does
it take to change a light bulb?
**About fifty – one to change the
bulb, the others to dance the conga
round the room.**

What lives on the Antarctic pack ice
and smells?
**A pong-uin.**

Why don't penguins holiday
in the British Isles?
**They're afraid of Wales.**

# Egg Yolks

Aiy! Stop it! You're cracking me up!

Which TV programme do unhatched chicks like best?
**The Eggs-Factor.**

How did Mumble feel when Memphis dropped his egg?
**Shell-shocked.**

What do you do with a penguin egg that won't hatch?
**Tell it to get cracking.**

**You know, I used to be really shy.**

Ju? No!

**It's true.
It took me a long time to come out of my shell ...**

What do you call a penguin in a shell suit?
**An egg.**

# Ice-breakers

What do you get if you cross
a snowman and a killer whale?
**Frostbite.**

Name ten animals from Antarctica.
**A penguin and nine seals.**

Lovelace,
why do I feel like
I am invisible?

Next!

How do penguins drink their cola?
**On the rocks.**

**Norma Jean:** How are you doing
in school, dear?
**Mumble:** I'm doing well in
everything except for my lessons!

Why was the Emperor penguin
chick thrown out by his father?
**For smoking in bed.**

# Seafood Jokes

> Don't be shellfish - share these with your brothers and sisters!

How much is a typical meal for a family of Emperor penguins?
**Six squid.**

**BABY SEAL:** Does your mum really regurgitate food for you?

**PENGUIN CHICK:** Yes, but she doesn't like to bring it up in company.

What do you call an Adelie penguin who spoils his friends' mealtimes?
**A krill-joy.**

Hey, *amigo* – do you know the best way to catch a fish?

*Sí* – have someone throw it to ju.

What did the Emperor penguin say to his mate when she regurgitated a flat fish?
**'What's a plaice like this doing in a nice girl like you?'**

# More Whale Jokes

Some of these are killers, my friends!

Why should you never tease whales about their weight?
**They tend to blubber.**

What do you get from a bad-tempered killer whale?
**As far away as possible.**

What do ju get if ju cross a baby penguin with a giant white whale?

I dunno.

Moby Chick.

What's a kilogram?
**A black and white whale that sings on your doorstep.**

What happens when orcas get together?
**They have a whale of a time.**

# Mumble's Top Five Zoo Survival Tips

**1. Don't play cards with the big cats. Some of them are cheetahs.**

2. If you like your fish toasted, pop it under the gorilla.

**3. Don't tease the elephants. They never forget.**

4. Keep your beak out of the chimpanzees' affairs. That's monkey business.

**5. Don't promise the crocodiles that you'll drop round for lunch.**

# Even More Penguin Jokes

What do you call a hungry 400-kilogram Leopard seal?

**Whatever it wants you to.**

What do you call a big
Antarctic dance party?
**A snow-ball.**

What's black and white and
plays the piano badly?
**A penguin with mittens on.**

Why don't polar bears
eat penguins?
**They can't get the wrappers off.**

What do you call a woman with
an emperor penguin on her head?
**Flo.**

# Emperor Land Best-sellers

**The Big Book of Heart Songs**
by Mel O'Dee

**The Antarctic Ocean**
by I. C. Waters

**Living at the Pole**
by R. U. Bonkas

**Penguin Life Cycles**
by Leah Negg

**Polar Bird Life**
by C. Gulls

**Navigating Antarctica**
by Noah Root
and Hugo d'Atway

**Penguin Plumage**
by Blake N. White

# Even More Than Before Penguin Jokes

Did you hear about the man who was planning to live in a penguin colony? **He got cold feet.**

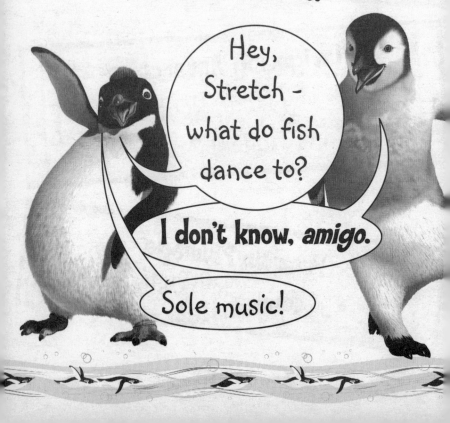

Hey, Stretch - what do fish dance to?

I don't know, *amigo.*

Sole music!

What brand of crisps do penguins eat?
**Squalkers.**

What's the difference between Emperor Land and a good Samaritan?
**One's an ice cap, the other's a nice chap.**

**NESTOR:** Hey, Ramon - which TV programme do whales like best?
**RAMON:** I dunno, muchacho.
**NESTOR:** Big Blubber!

What's black and white, teo metres tall and has a bolt through its neck?
**Penguinstein.**